सीताय

MW01357293

Nama-Ramayanam Legacy Book

-

Endowment of Devotion

:

Embellish it with Your

Rama Namas

& Present it to Someone You Love

::

नाम-रामायणम व राम-नाम माला

Belongs to ______________________________

Presented to ______________________________

____

____

Published by: RAMA-Nama Journals
(an Imprint of e1i1 Corporation)

Title: Nama-Ramayanam Legacy Book - Endowment of Devotion
Sub-Title: Embellish it with your Rama Namas & present it to someone you love

Author/Designer: Sushma

Parts of this book have been derived/inspired from our other publication:
"Rama Hymns" (Authored by Sushma)

Identifiers

ISBN: **978-1-945739-30-9** (Paperback)
ISBN: **978-1-945739-95-8** (Hardcover)

—o—

—o—

www.e1i1.com -- www.OnlyRama.com
email: e1i1*books*e1i1@gmail.com

⌘⌘⌘⌘⌘⌘⌘⌘⌘⌘⌘⌘⌘⌘⌘⌘⌘⌘⌘⌘⌘⌘⌘⌘⌘⌘⌘⌘⌘⌘⌘⌘⌘⌘⌘
⌘⌘⌘⌘⌘⌘⌘⌘⌘⌘⌘⌘⌘⌘⌘⌘⌘⌘⌘⌘⌘⌘⌘⌘⌘⌘⌘⌘⌘⌘⌘⌘⌘⌘⌘

कलिजुग केवल हरि गुन गाहा । गावत नर पावहिं भव थाहा ॥

kalijuga kevala hari guna gāhā, gāvata nara pāvahiṁ bhava thāhā.

कलिजुग जोग न जग्य न ग्याना । एक अधार राम गुन गाना ॥

kalijuga joga na jagya na gyānā, eka adhāra rāma guna gānā.

The only appointed means for the Kali-Yuga is singing the praises of the Lord—just following that simple path people are able to cross this turbulent worldly life. In this Yuga neither Yoga nor Yagya nor Wisdom is of much avail—the only hope is in chanting the Holy-Name राम राम राम.

⌘⌘⌘⌘⌘

In all the four ages; in all times, past, present, or future; in the three spheres of creation—anyone that repeats the name **राम** becomes blessed. The name of Rāma is like the Tree-of-Heaven, and is the centre of all that is good in the world, and whoever meditates upon it verily becomes transformed—even the vile-most turn holy. As Narasingh became manifest to destroy Hiranyākashyap, the enemy of gods, in order to protect Prahlād—so is the Name of Rāma **राम** for the destruction of the wicked and protection of devout.

The chanting of Rāma-Nāma is a direct way to liberation. By repeating the **राम** name—whether in joy or in sadness, in activity or in repose—bliss is diffused all around. According to the Vedas, just as the Sun dispels darkness, the chanting of Rāma-Nāma dispels all the evils and obstacles of life. The Rāma Nāma cures agony and showers the blessings of God; all righteous wishes get fulfilled; jealousy and pride disappear; life becomes imbued with satisfaction and peace; all of life's needs fall in place naturally—just like a miracle of nature guiding nature's forces. You may not always get what you want in the exact same form, but the Rāma-Nāma will sanctify things and bring to you the same needed happiness and bliss in a much more refined and lasting way. Life truly becomes filled with tranquility. With the Rāma-Nāma, an immense sense of inner spiritual wellbeing is experienced apart from a gain of external material happiness.

⌘⌘⌘⌘⌘

राम नाम मनिदीप धरु जीह देहरीं द्वार ।

rāma nāma manidīpa dharu jīha deharīṁ dvāra,

तुलसी भीतर बाहेरहुँ जौं चाहसि उजिआर ॥

tulasī bhītara bāherahuṁ jauṁ cāhasi ujiāra.

O Tulsīdās, place the luminous gem in the shape of the divine name 'Rāma' on the tongue—which is at the threshold, the doorway to the inside—and you will have light both on inside and outside. (i.e. Always chant **राम**, and its radiance will illumine your mind, body, life—all around, everywhere, inside out.)

—⌘⌘⌘⌘⌘⌘⌘⌘⌘—

Rāma Jayam: Journal for writing the Holy-Name **राम**. Once embellished with your Rāma-Nāmas, this journal will become a priceless treasure which you can present to your loved ones—an unparalleled gift of love, labor, caring, wishing, and above all—Devotion.

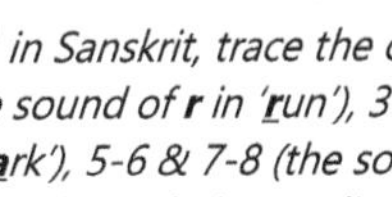

To write **राम** *in Sanskrit, trace the contours 1-2 (which is the sound of* ***r*** *in '****r****un'), 3-4 (the sound* ***a*** *in '****a****rk'), 5-6 & 7-8 (the sound* ***m*** *in '****m****ust') and lastly mark the top line 9-10. Please note the pronunciation:* **राम** *rhymes with calm.*

शुद्धब्रह्मपरात्पर

राम

suddha

brahma

parātpara

rāma

राम राम

-- बालकाण्डः -- bālakāṇḍaḥ --

॥ **शुद्धब्रह्मपरात्पर राम** ॥

śuddhabrahmaparātpara rāma .1.

Behold Rāma—of the nature of pure Braham, who is the Supreme-One, second to none.

Dt: ______________________

कालात्मक

परमेश्वर राम

kālātmaka

param

eśvara rāma

॥ **कालात्मकपरमेश्वर राम** ॥

kālātmakaparameśvara rāma .2.

Behold Rāma—Sovereign Godhead, the embodiment of Eternal Time.

शेषतल्प

सुखनिद्रित राम

śesa talpa

sukha nidrita

rāma

॥ शेषतल्पसुखनिद्रित राम ॥

śeṣatalpasukhanidrita rāma .3.

Behold Rāma—who slumbers joyously on the bed made of serpent Shesha Naga.

Dt: ____________________

ब्रह्माद्यमर

प्रार्थित राम

brahmādy

amara

prārthita

rāma

॥ ब्रह्माद्यमरप्रार्थित राम ॥

brahmādyamara prārthita rāma .4.

Behold Rāma—whose Lotus Feet are venerated by Brahmmā and other divinities—with a view to attaining ever-lasting life.

चण्डकिरण

कुलमण्डन राम

caṇḍa kiraṇa

kula

maṇḍana

rāma

॥ **चण्डकिरणकुलमण्डन राम** ॥

caṇḍakiraṇakulamaṇḍana rāma .5.

Behold Rāma—the shining Jewel of the Solar-Dynasty.

Dt: ____________________

श्रीमद्दशरथ
नन्दन राम

śrīmad
daśaratha
nandana
rāma

|| श्रीमद्दशरथनन्दन राम ||

śrīmaddaśarathanandana rāma .6.

Behold Rāma—the illustrious Son of King Dashrath.

कौसल्या

सुखवर्धन राम

kausalyā

sukha

vardhana

rāma

॥ **कौसल्यासुखवर्धन राम** ॥

kausalyāsukhavardhana rāma .7.

Behold Rāma—who exceedingly amplifies His mother Kausalyā's joy.

Dt: ______________________

विश्वामित्र

प्रियधन राम

viśvāmitra

priya dhana

rāma

॥ **विश्वामित्रप्रियधन राम** ॥

viśvāmitrapriyadhana rāma .8.

Behold Rāma—the very precious treasure of Sage Vishwāmitra.

घोरताटका

घातक राम

ghoratāṭakā

ghātaka rāma

राम राम

॥ घोरताटकाघातक राम ॥

ghoratāṭakāghātaka rāma .9.

Behold Rāma—Slayer of Tādaka, the terrible fiend.

Dt: ____________________

मारीचादि निपातक राम

mārīcādi nipātaka rāma

|| मारीचादिनिपातक राम ||

mārīcādinipātaka rāma .10.

Behold Rāma—who wrought the downfall of Māricha and other Demons.

कौशिकमख

संरक्षक राम

kauśika

makha

saṁrakṣaka

rāma

॥ **कौशिकमखसंरक्षक राम** ॥

kauśikamakhasaṁrakṣaka rāma .11.

Behold Rāma—the Guardian of the Yagya of Sage Vishwāmitra.

Dt: ____________________

श्रीमदहल्योद्धारक

राम

śrīmad
ahalyoddhāraka
rāma

॥ श्रीमदहल्योद्धारक राम ॥

śrīmadahalyoddhāraka rāma .12.

Behold Rāma—as He imparts redemption to the venerable Ahalyā.

गौतममुनि

संपूजित राम

gautama

muni

saṁpūjita

rāma

राम राम

॥ गौतममुनिसंपूजित राम ॥

gautamamunisaṁpūjita rāma .13.

Behold Rāma—being worshipped by Muni Gautam.

Dt: ____________________

राम
राम
राम
राम
राम
राम
राम
राम
राम
राम
राम
राम
राम
राम
राम
राम
राम
राम
राम
राम
राम
राम
राम
राम

सुरमुनिवर गण

संस्तुत राम

suramunivara

gaṇa saṁstuta

rāma

॥ सुरमुनिवरगणसंस्तुत राम ॥

suramunivaragaṇasaṁstuta rāma .14

Behold Rāma—who is ever praised by the gods and hosts of sages

नाविकधाविक

मृदुपद राम

nāvika

dhāvika

mṛdupada

rāma

राम राम

॥ नाविकधाविकमृदुपद राम ॥

nāvikadhāvikamṛdupada rāma .15.

Behold Rāma—whose gentle feet are being washed by the Boatman.

Dt: ____________________

राम
राम
राम
राम
राम
राम
राम
राम
राम
राम
राम
राम
राम
राम
राम
राम
राम
राम
राम
राम
राम
राम
राम

मिथिलापुर
जनमोहक राम

mithilāpura
jana mohaka
rāma

॥ मिथिलापुरजनमोहक राम ॥

mithilāpurajanamohaka rāma .16.

Behold Rāma—the Lordly prince who has so captivated the citizenry of Mithila.

विदेहमानस

रञ्जक राम

videhamānasa

rañjaka rāma

॥ **विदेहमानसरञ्जक राम** ॥

videhamānasarañjaka rāma .17.

Behold Rāma—who has enhanced the glory of King Janaka.

Dt: ______________________

त्र्यंबककार्मुख

भञ्जक राम

tryaṁbaka
kārmukha
bhañjaka
rāma

॥ त्र्यंबककार्मुखभञ्जक राम ॥

tryaṁbakakārmukhabhañjaka rāma .18.

Behold Rāma—as He breaks the Bow of the Three-Eyed Shiva.

सीतार्पित वरमालिक राम

sītārpita varamālika rāma

॥ **सीतार्पितवरमालिक राम** ॥

sītārpitavaramālika rāma .19.

Behold Sītā—who offers Her victory-garland to Rāma in matrimony.

राम राम

Dt: ____________________

कृतवैवाहिक
कौतुक राम

krtavaivāhika
kautuka rāma

॥ कृतवैवाहिककौतुक राम ॥

kṛtavaivāhikakautuka rāma .20.

Behold Rāma—as He enacts the sport of marriage ceremony.

भार्गवदर्प

विनाशक राम

bhārgava

darpa

vināśaka

rāma

राम राम

॥ भार्गवदर्पविनाशक राम ॥

bhārgavadarpavināśaka rāma .21.

Behold Rāma—now seen destroying the pride of Parshurāma.

Dt: ____________________

श्रीमदयोध्या

पालक राम

śrīmad

ayodhyā

pālaka rāma

॥ श्रीमदयोध्यापालक राम ॥

śrīmadayodhyāpālaka rāma .22.

Behold Rāma—the Lord-God, Ayodhya's Empyreal Sovereign.

राम राम जय राजा राम - राम राम जय सीता राम

rāma rāma jaya rājā rāma - rāma rāma jaya sītā rāma

अगणितगुणगण भूषित राम

aganita guṇagaṇa bhūṣita rāma

अयोध्याकाण्डः ayodhyākāṇḍaḥ

॥ अगणितगुणगणभूषित राम ॥

aganitaguṇagaṇabhūṣita rāma .23.

Behold Rāma—who is graced with immeasurable virtues.

Dt: ____________________

अवनीतनया
कामित राम

avanītanayā
kāmita rāma

॥ अवनीतनयाकामित राम ॥

avanītanayākāmita rāma .24.

Behold Rāma—the heart's desire of Sītā: Daughter-of-the-Earth.

राकाचन्द्र
समानन राम

rākācandra
samānana
rāma

॥ **राकाचन्द्रसमानन राम** ॥

rākācandrasamānana rāma .25.

Behold Rāma—whose resplendent face is like the full Moon.

Dt: ______________________

पितृवाक्याश्रित कानन राम

pitṛvākyāśrita kānana rāma

॥ पितृवाक्याश्रितकानन राम ॥

pitṛvākyāśritakānana rāma .26.

Behold Rāma—who leaves for exile to the forest in order to honor His father's words.

प्रियगुहविनि
वेदितपद राम

priyaguha
vinivedita
pada rāma

॥ प्रियगुहविनिवेदितपद राम ॥

priyaguhavinivेditapada rāma .27.

Behold Rāma—unto whose holy feet Guha offers himself up as a cherished devotee.

Dt: ______________________

राम
राम
राम
राम
राम
राम
राम
राम
राम
राम
राम
राम
राम
राम
राम
राम
राम
राम
राम
राम
राम
राम
राम
राम
राम

तत्क्षालित

निजमृदुपद राम

tatkṣālitanija

mṛdupada

rāma

॥ तत्क्षालितनिजमृदुपद राम ॥

tatkṣālitanijamṛdupada rāma .28.

Behold Rāma—whose gentle feet Guha has the good fortune to lave.

भरद्वाज

मुखानन्दक राम

bharadvāja

mukhā

nandaka

rāma

राम राम

॥ भरद्वाजमुखानन्दक राम ॥

bharadvājamukhānandaka rāma .29.

Behold Rāma—whose presence makes Sage Bharadwaja face lighten up with supreme joy.

Dt: ______________________

चित्रकूटाद्रि
निकेतन राम

citrakūṭādri
niketana
rāma

॥ चित्रकूटाद्रिनिकेतन राम ॥

citrakūṭādriniketana rāma .30.

Behold Rāma—making Mount Chitrakut His habitat in the woods.

दशरथसन्तत
चिन्तित राम

daśaratha
santata cintita
rāma

॥ दशरथसन्ततचिन्तित राम ॥

daśarathasantatacintita rāma .31.

Behold Rāma—ever mindful of Dashratha, His father, during the exile.

Dt: ______________________________

कैकेयीतनयार्थित

राम

kaikeyī

tanayārthita

rāma

॥ कैकेयीतनयार्थित राम ॥

kaikeyītanayārthita rāma .32.

Behold Rāma—being eagerly besought by the son of Kaikayi to come return to His Kingdom.

विरचितनिजपितृ

कर्मक राम

viracita nija

pitṛ karmaka

rāma

॥ विरचितनिजपितृकर्मक राम ॥

viracitanijapitṛkarmaka rāma .33.

Behold Rāma—seen performing the last rites of his sire—King Dashrath.

Dt: ______________________

राम
राम
राम
राम
राम
राम
राम
राम
राम
राम
राम
राम
राम
राम
राम
राम
राम
राम
राम
राम
राम
राम
राम

भरतार्पितनिज

पादुक राम

bharatārpita

nija pāduka

rāma

॥ भरतार्पितनिजपादुक राम ॥

bharatārpitanijapāduka rāma .34.

Behold Rāma—as He bestows His own Padukā to brother Bharat.

दण्डकावनजन

पावन राम

daṇḍakāvana

jana pāvana

rāma

अरण्यकाण्डः araṇyakāṇḍaḥ

॥ दण्डकावनजनपावन राम ॥

daṇḍakāvanajanapāvana rāma .35.

Behold Rāma—who has sanctified the Dandak Forest and the habitants therein.

Dt: ____________________

दुष्टविराध
विनाशन राम
duṣṭavirādha
vināśana
rāma

॥ दुष्टविराधविनाशन राम ॥

duṣṭavirādhavināśana rāma .36.

Behold Rāma—who has destroyed Viradha the wicked demon.

शरभङ्ग
सुतीक्ष्णार्चित राम

śarabhaṅga
sutīkṣṇ
ārcita rāma

॥ **शरभङ्गसुतीक्ष्णार्चित राम** ॥

śarabhaṅgasutīkṣṇārcita rāma .37.

Behold Rāma—being worshipped by the sages Sharabhang and Sutīkshan.

Dt: ____________________

अगस्त्यानुग्रह

वर्धित राम

agasty
ānugraha
vardhita rāma

॥ अगस्त्यानुग्रहवर्धित राम ॥

agastyānugrahavardhita rāma .38.

Behold Rāma— augmented with the blessings and grace of sage Agastya.

गृध्राधिपसंसेवित राम

gṛdhrādhipa saṁsevita rāma

॥ गृध्राधिपसंसेवित राम ॥

gṛdhrādhipasaṁsevita rāma .39.

Behold Rāma—being honored by Jatāyu, the vulture-king.

Dt: ____________________

राम
राम
राम
राम
राम
राम
राम
राम
राम
राम
राम
राम
राम
राम
राम
राम
राम
राम
राम
राम
राम
राम
राम
राम

पञ्चवटीतट
सुस्थित राम

pañcavaṭī
taṭa susthita
rāma

॥ पञ्चवटीतटसुस्थित राम ॥

pañcavaṭītaṭasusthita rāma .40.

Behold Rāma—dwelling on the banks of the river at Panchavati.

शूर्पणखार्त्ति
विधायक राम

śūrpaṇakh
ārtti
vidhāyaka
rāma

|| शूर्पणखार्त्तिविधायक राम ||
śūrpaṇakhārttividhāyaka rāma .41.
Behold Rāma—as He visits punishment upon Surpanakha for her wicked deeds.

खरदूषणमुख

सूदक राम

kharadūṣaṇa
mukha
sūdaka rāma

॥ **खरदूषणमुखसूदक राम** ॥

kharadūṣaṇamukhasūdaka rāma .42.

Behold Rāma—seen effacing demons Khara and Dushana from the world.

सीताप्रिय
हरिणानुग राम
sītāpriya
hariṇānuga
rāma

॥ सीताप्रियहरिणानुग राम ॥

sītāpriyahariṇānuga rāma .43.

Behold Rāma—as He pursues the deer which Sītā has wished for herself.

Dt: ____________________

राम
राम
राम
राम
राम
राम
राम
राम
राम
राम
राम
राम
राम
राम
राम
राम
राम
राम
राम
राम
राम
राम
राम
राम

मारीचार्ति
कृदाशुग राम
māricārti
kṛdāśuga
rāma

मारीचार्तिकृदाशुग राम ॥

māricārtikṛdāśuga rāma .44.

Behold Rāma—who visits pain with an arrow upon Marich for his faulty deeds.

विनष्टसीतान्वेषक

राम

vinasṭa sītān veṣaka rāma

॥ **विनष्टसीतान्वेषक राम** ॥

vinaṣṭasītānveṣaka rāma .45.

Behold Rāma—seen earnestly searching for Sītā, His beloved, who is found missing.

Dt: ____________________

राम
राम
राम
राम
राम
राम
राम
राम
राम
राम
राम
राम
राम
राम
राम
राम
राम
राम
राम
राम
राम
राम
राम
राम

गृध्राधिप

गति दायक राम

gṛdhrādhipa

gati dāyaka

rāma

॥ गृध्राधिपगतिदायक राम ॥

gṛdhrādhipagatidāyaka rāma .46.

Behold Rāma—imparting emancipation to Jatāyu, the vulture-king.

शबरीदत्त

फलाशन राम

śabarīdatta

phalāśana

rāma

॥ शबरीदत्तफलाशन राम ॥

śabarīdattaphalāśana rāma .47.

Behold Rāma—partaking of the fruit offerings made by the woman sage Shabarī.

Dt: ____________________

राम
राम
राम
राम
राम
राम
राम
राम
राम
राम
राम
राम
राम
राम
राम
राम
राम
राम
राम
राम
राम
राम
राम
राम

कबन्धबाहुच्छेदन

राम

kabandha bāhu cchedana rāma

॥ कबन्धबाहुच्छेदन राम ॥

kabandhabāhucchedana rāma .48.

Behold Rāma—severing the arms of Kabandh, the monster fiend.

राम राम जय राजा राम - राम राम जय सीता राम

rāma rāma jaya rājā rāma - rāma rāma jaya sītā rāma

हनुमत्सेवित
निजपद राम

hanumat
sevita
nijapada
rāma

किष्किन्धाकाण्डः kiṣkindhākāṇḍaḥ

॥ हनुमत्सेवितनिजपद राम ॥

hanumatsevitanijapada rāma .49.

Behold Rāma—King of Kings, whose Holy Feet are being served by Hanumān, the monkey chief.

Dt: ______________________

राम राम

नतसुग्रीवाभीष्टद राम

nata sugrīv ābhīṣṭada rāma

॥ **नतसुग्रीवाभीष्टद राम** ॥

natasugrīvābhīṣṭada rāma .50.

Behold Rāma—granting the prayers of Sugrīva, who has arrived bowing to Him, seeking refuge.

गर्वितवालि

संहारक राम

garvita vāli

saṁhāraka

rāma

राम राम

Shri-Rama-Namayana

॥ गर्वितवालिसंहारक राम ॥

garvitavālisaṁhāraka rāma .51.

Behold Rāma—who has put to death Vāli, the haughty monkey-king.

Dt: ____________________

राम
राम
राम
राम
राम
राम
राम
राम
राम
राम
राम
राम
राम
राम
राम
राम
राम
राम
राम
राम
राम
राम
राम

वानरदूत प्रेषक राम

vānaradūta preṣaka rāma

॥ **वानरदूतप्रेषक राम** ॥

vānaradūtapreṣaka rāma .52.

Behold Rāma—who has sent monkeys as emissaries in search of Sītā.

हितकरलक्ष्मण
संयुत राम
hitakara
lakṣmaṇa
saṁyuta rāma

राम राम

॥ हितकरलक्ष्मणसंयुत राम ॥

hitakaralakṣmaṇasaṁyuta rāma .53.

Behold Rāma—with Lakshman dwelling alongside Him, serving devotedly.

कपिवरसन्तत संस्मृत राम

kapivara santata saṁsmṛta rāma

सुन्दरकाण्डः sundarakāṇḍaḥ

॥ कपिवरसन्ततसंस्मृत राम ॥

kapivarasantatasaṁsmṛta rāma .54.

Behold Rāma—who is continually thought upon by Hanumān, the most-excellent amongst the monkeys.

तद्गतिविघ्न
ध्वंसक राम
tad gati
vighna
dhvaṁsaka
rāma

॥ तद्गतिविघ्नध्वंसक राम ॥

tadgativighnadhvaṁsaka rāma .55.

Behold Rāma—as He removes all impediments and obstacles to the swiftness of Hanumān's rapid speed.

Dt: ____________________

राम राम

राम
राम
राम
राम
राम
राम
राम
राम
राम
राम
राम
राम
राम
राम
राम
राम
राम
राम
राम
राम
राम
राम
राम

सीताप्राणा धारक राम

sītā prāṇā dhāraka rāma

॥ सीताप्राणाधारक राम ॥

sītāprāṇādhāraka rāma .56.

Behold Rāma—the support and sustenance of the life of Sītā in captivity.

दुष्टदशाननदूषित

राम

duṣṭa

daśānana

dūṣita rāma

॥ **दुष्टदशाननदूषित राम** ॥

duṣṭadaśānanadūṣita rāma .57.

Behold Rāma—being affronted & marred by the wicked Ten-Headed Rāvan.

Dt: ____________________

शिष्टहनूमद्भूषित

राम

śiṣṭa

hanūmad

bhūṣita rāma

॥ शिष्टहनूमद्भूषित राम ॥

śiṣṭahanūmadbhūṣita rāma .58.

Behold Rāma—being praised & graced by the Honorable Hanumān.

सीतावेदित
काकावन राम
sītā vedita
kākāvana
rāma

राम राम

॥ सीतावेदितकाकावन राम ॥

sītāveditakākāvana rāma .59.

Behold Rāma—as He hears of the Kakasur incident in woods which was conveyed to Him by Shrī Sītā.

Dt: ______

कृतचूडामणि
दर्शन राम
kṛta
cūḍāmaṇi
darśana rāma

॥ कृतचूडामणिदर्शन राम ॥

kṛtacūḍāmaṇidarśana rāma .60.

Behold Rāma—beholding the head-crest chudāmani of Shrī Sītā.

कपिवर वचनाश्वासित राम

kapivara vacanāśvāsita rāma

॥ कपिवरवचनाश्वासित राम ॥

kapivaravacanāśvāsita rāma .61.

Behold Rāma—being comforted by the words of Shrī Hanumān, the wisest amongst the monkeys.

राम राम

रावणनिधन
प्रस्थित राम

rāvaṇa nidhana
prasthita
rāma

युद्धकाण्डः yuddhakāṇḍaḥ

॥ रावणनिधनप्रस्थित राम ॥

rāvaṇanidhanaprasthita rāma .62.

Behold Rāma—as He sallies forth to decimate Rāvan, the demon king.

वानरसैन्य
समावृत राम

vānarasainya
samāvṛta
rāma

॥ **वानरसैन्यसमावृत राम** ॥

vānarasainyasamāvṛta rāma .63.

Behold Rāma—accompanied by the army of bears and monkeys.

Dt: ____________________

राम
राम
राम
राम
राम
राम
राम
राम
राम
राम
राम
राम
राम
राम
राम
राम
राम
राम
राम
राम
राम
राम
राम

शोषित
सरिदीशार्थित
राम

śoṣita saridī
śārthita rāma

॥ शोषितसरिदीशार्थित राम ॥

śoṣitasaridīśārthita rāma .64.

Behold Rāma—being importuned by the king of oceans when He asks It to make way—and then makes ready to dry up the sea.

विभीषणाभय

दायक राम

vibhīṣṇ

ābhaya

dāyaka rāma

राम राम

॥ विभीषणाभयदायक राम ॥

vibhīṣṇābhayadāyaka rāma .65.

Behold Rāma—who confers fearlessness upon Vibhīshan who has come seeking sanctuary.

Dt: ____________________

पर्वतसेतु
निबन्धक राम

parvata setu
nibandhaka
rāma

॥ पर्वतसेतुनिबन्धक राम ॥

parvatasetunibandhaka rāma .66.

Behold Rāma—who has spanned a bridge of rocks across the ocean.

कुम्भकर्ण शिरश्छेदक राम

kumbhakarṇa śiraśchedaka rāma

॥ कुम्भकर्णशिरश्छेदक राम ॥

kumbhakarṇaśiraśchedaka rāma .67.

Behold Rāma—as He beheads Kumbhkaran in combat.

राक्षससङ्घ

विमर्दक राम

rākṣasa

saṅgha

vimardaka

rāma

॥ राक्षससङ्घविमर्दक राम ॥

rākṣasasaṅghavimardaka rāma .68.

Behold Rāma—crushing the army of demons on the battleground.

अहिमहिरावण
चारण राम

ahimahi
rāvaṇa cāraṇa
rāma

राम राम

॥ अहिमहिरावणचारण राम ॥

ahimahirāvaṇacāraṇa rāma .69.

Behold Rāma—upon whom Ahi-Mahi Rāvana spied taking the guise of musician.

संहृतदशमुख
रावण राम

samhṛta
daśamukha
rāvaṇa rāma

॥ संहृतदशमुखरावण राम ॥

saṁhṛtadaśamukharāvaṇa rāma .70.

Behold Rāma—as He kills the Ten-Headed Rāvan in the battlefield.

विधिभवमुख

सुरसंस्तुत राम

vidhibhava
mukha sura
saṁstuta
rāma

॥ विधिभवमुखसुरसंस्तुत राम ॥

vidhibhavamukhasurasaṁstuta rāma .71

Behold Rāma—being worshiped by Brahmmā, Shiva and other Divinities.

Dt: ______________________

राम राम

स्वस्थितदशरथ

वीक्षित राम

svasthita

daśaratha

vīkṣita rāma

॥ स्वस्थितदशरथवीक्षित राम ॥

svasthitadaśarathavīkṣita rāma .72.

Behold Rāma—whose divine deeds are being witnessed by father Dashratha from the Heavens.

सीतादर्शन
मोदित राम

sītādarśana
modita rāma

॥ **सीतादर्शनमोदित राम** ॥

sītādarśanamodita rāma .73.

Behold Rāma—as He beholds with delight Shrī Sītā after the battle is won.

Dt: ______________________

अभिषिक्त

विभीषणनत राम

abhiṣikta

vibhīṣaṇanata

rāma

॥ अभिषिक्तविभीषणनत राम ॥

abhiṣiktavibhīṣaṇanata rāma .74.

Behold Rāma—being reverentially saluted by Vibhīshan after his own corronation.

पुष्पकयानारोहण

राम

puṣpaka yānārohaṇa rāma

॥ **पुष्पकयानारोहण राम** ॥

puṣpakayānārohaṇa rāma .75.

Behold Rāma—while He boards the aerial Pushpaka Vimana to return to Ayodhya, His Kingdom.

Dt: ______________________

भरद्वाजादि
निषेवण राम
bharadvājādi
niṣevaṇa
rāma

॥ भरद्वाजादिनिषेवण राम ॥

bharadvājādiniṣevaṇa rāma .76.

Behold Rāma—being served by sage Bharadwaja and the other sages.

भरतप्राणप्रियकर

राम

bharata prāṇa priyakara rāma

॥ भरतप्राणप्रियकर राम ॥

bharatapraāṇapriyakara rāma .77.

Behold Rāma—who brings joy to Bharta's life upon His return.

Dt: ____________________

राम
राम
राम
राम
राम
राम
राम
राम
राम
राम
राम
राम
राम
राम
राम
राम
राम
राम
राम
राम
राम
राम
राम
राम

साकेतपुरी भूषण राम

sāketapurī bhūṣaṇa rāma

॥ **साकेतपुरीभूषण राम** ॥

sāketapurībhūṣaṇa rāma .78.

Behold Rāma—the adornment of the city of Sāket.

सकलस्वीय
समानस राम
sakalasvīya
samānasa
rāma

राम राम

॥ सकलस्वीयसमानस राम ॥

sakalasvīyasamānasa rāma .79.

Behold Rāma—being welcomed and venerated by the citizenry of Ayodhyā.

Dt: ____________________

रत्नलसत्पीठा

स्थित राम

ratnala

satpīṭhāsthita

rāma

॥ रत्नलसत्पीठास्थित राम ॥

ratnalasatpīṭhāsthita rāma .80.

Behold Rāma—seated on the Royal Throne embellished with shining jewels.

पट्टाभिषेकालंकृत

राम

paṭṭābhiṣek
ālaṁkṛta
rāma

॥ पट्टाभिषेकालंकृत राम ॥

paṭṭābhiṣekālaṁkṛta rāma .81.

Behold Rāma—adorned with the Royal Robes and Crown upon His coronation.

Dt: ______________________

पार्थिवकुल

सम्मानित राम

pārthivakula

sammānita

rāma

॥ पार्थिवकुलसम्मानित राम ॥

pārthivakulasammānita rāma .82.

Behold Rāma—being honoured by the Assembly of Kings

विभीषणार्पित

रङ्क राम

vibhīṣaṇ
ārpita
raṅgaka rāma

॥ **विभीषणार्पितरङ्क राम** ॥

vibhīṣaṇārpitaraṅgaka rāma .83.

Behold Rāma—as He confers the idol of Shrī Ranganātha to Vibhishana.

Dt: ______________________

कीशकुला

नुग्रहकर राम

kīśakul

ānugraha

kara rāma

॥ कीशकुलानुग्रहकर राम ॥

kīśakulānugrahakara rāma .84.

Behold Rāma—showering His benediction upon the host of Monkeys.

सकलजीव संरक्षक राम

sakala jīva saṁrakṣaka rāma

॥ **सकलजीवसंरक्षक राम** ॥

sakalajīvasaṁrakṣaka rāma .85.

Behold Rāma—the Guardian of all beings.

Dt: ____________________

राम
राम
राम
राम
राम
राम
राम
राम
राम
राम
राम
राम
राम
राम
राम
राम
राम
राम
राम
राम
राम
राम

समस्तलोकाधारक

राम

samasta

lokādhāraka

rāma

॥ **समस्तलोकाधारक राम** ॥

samastalokādhāraka rāma .86.

Behold Rāma—the Sustainer of all the worlds.

आगत मुनिगण संस्तुत राम

āgata munigaṇa saṁstuta rāma

उत्तरकाण्डः uttarakāṇḍaḥ

॥ आगत मुनिगण संस्तुत राम ॥

āgata munigaṇa saṁstuta rāma .87.

Behold Rāma—being revered by the visiting host of Munis.

Dt: ____________________

विश्रुतदशकण्ठोद्भव

राम

viśruta
daśakaṇṭh
odbhava
rāma

॥ विश्रुतदशकण्ठोद्भव राम ॥

viśrutadaśakaṇṭhodbhava rāma .88.

Behold Rāma—as He hears the story of the origin of the Ten-Faced Rāvan.

सितालिङ्गन निर्वृत राम

sitāliṅgana nirvṛta rāma

॥ सितालिङ्गननिर्वृत राम ॥

sitāliṅgananirvṛta rāma .89.

Behold Rāma—living happily, united with Sītā.

Dt: ______________

नीतिसुरक्षित

जनपद राम

nītisurakṣita

janapada

rāma

॥ **नीतिसुरक्षितजनपद राम** ॥

nītisurakṣitajanapada rāma .90.

Behold Rāma—who protects His Sovereignity through Dharma—the moral-precept.

विपिनत्याजित
जनकज राम

vipina tyājita
janakaja rāma

॥ **विपिनत्याजितजनकज राम** ॥

vipinatyājitajanakaja rāma .91.

Behold Rāma—who has to abandon the daughter of Janak into the woods.

Dt: ____________________

राम
राम
राम
राम
राम
राम
राम
राम
राम
राम
राम
राम
राम
राम
राम
राम
राम
राम
राम
राम
राम
राम
राम
राम

कारितलवणासुर

वध राम

kārita

lavaṇāsura

vadha rāma

॥ **कारितलवणासुरवध राम** ॥

kāritalavaṇāsuravadha rāma .92.

Behold Rāma—as He brings about destruction of the Lavanasura Demon.

स्वर्गतशाम्बुक

संस्तुत राम

svargata

śambuka

saṁstuta

rāma

॥ स्वर्गतशम्बुक संस्तुत राम ॥

svargataśambuka saṁstuta rāma .93.

Behold Rāma—being praised by Shambuka, whom He sent to the Heavens.

Dt: ______________________

राम राम

स्वतनयकुशलव
नन्दित राम

svatanaya
kuśa lava
nandita rāma

॥ **स्वतनयकुशलवनन्दित राम** ॥

svatanayakuśalavanandita rāma .94.

Behold Rāma—jubilant by the sight of His sons Kusha and Lava.

अश्वमेधक्रतु
दीक्षित राम

aśvamedha
kratu dīkṣita
rāma

॥ **अश्वमेधक्रतुदीक्षित राम** ॥

aśvamedhakratudīkṣita rāma .95.

Behold Rāma—performing the sacrifices of Ashwamedha Yagya, proper to a King.

कालावेदित

सुरपद राम

kālāvedita

surapada

rāma

॥ कालावेदितसुरपद राम ॥

kālāveditasurapada rāma .96.

Behold Rāma—as He is reminded of His Divine-Abode from Kāla, the mighty Time.

आयोध्यकजन

मुक्तित राम

āyodhyaka

jana muktita

rāma

॥ **आयोध्यकजनमुक्तित राम** ॥

āyodhyakajanamuktita rāma .97.

Behold Rāma—conferring salvation upon all the inhabitants of Ayodhyā.

Dt: ______________________

राम राम

विधिमुखविभुदा
नन्दक राम

vidhimukha
vibhudā
nandaka
rāma

॥ विधिमुखविभुदानन्दक राम ॥

vidhimukhavibhudānandaka rāma .98.

Behold Rāma—who causes the faces of Brahmmā and other gods to brighten up with joy.

तेजोमय

निजरूपक राम

tejomaya nija

rūpaka rāma

॥ तेजोमयनिजरूपक राम ॥

tejomayanijarūpaka rāma .99.

Behold Rāma—who has assumed His own resplendent Divine-Form—fiery and gleaming.

Dt: ______________________

संसृतिबन्ध

विमोच्चक राम

samsrti
bandha
vimocaka
rāma

॥ संसृतिबन्धविमोचक राम ॥

saṁsṛtibandhavimocaka rāma .100.

Behold Rāma—who releases one from all the bondages of worldly existence.

धर्मस्थापन

तत्पर राम

dharma

sthāpana

tatpara rāma

॥ धर्मस्थापनतत्पर राम ॥

dharmasthāpanatatpara rāma .101.

Behold Rāma—ever ready to establish Dharma on Earth.

राम राम

Dt: ____________________

भक्तिपरायण

मुक्तिद राम

bhakti

parāyaṇa

muktida rāma

॥ भक्तिपरायणमुक्तिद राम ॥

bhaktiparāyaṇamuktida rāma .102.

Behold Rāma—giving salvation to Devotees that are completely dependent upon Him in thoughts, words, deeds.

सर्वंचराचर

पालक राम

sarva carācara

pālaka rāma

॥ सर्वंचराचरपालक राम ॥

sarvacarācarapālaka rāma .103.

Behold Rāma—the Guardian of all beings, moving and non-moving.

Dt: ______________________

सर्वभवामय
वारक राम

sarva
bhavāmaya
vāraka rāma

॥ सर्वभवामयवारक राम ॥

sarvabhavāmayavāraka rāma .104.

Behold Rāma—who takes His Devotees beyond the worldly dualities.

वैकुण्ठालय

संस्थित राम

vaikuṇṭhālaya

saṁsthita

rāma

॥ वैकुण्ठालयसंस्थित राम ॥

vaikuṇṭhālayasaṁsthita rāma .105.

Behold Rāma—ever established in His Divine Abode at Vaikuntha.

Dt: ____________________

राम
राम
राम
राम
राम
राम
राम
राम
राम
राम
राम
राम
राम
राम
राम
राम
राम
राम
राम
राम
राम
राम
राम
राम
राम

नित्यानन्द पदस्थित राम

nityānanda padasthita rāma

॥ नित्यानन्दपदस्थित राम ॥

nityānandapadasthita rāma .106.

Behold Rāma—forever established as the Divine Godhead of Eternal Bliss.

राम राम जय

राजा राम

rāma rāma

jaya

rājā rāma

॥ राम राम जय राजा राम ॥

rāma rāma jaya rājā rāma .107.

Sing the glories of the Almighty—Raja Rāma.

Dt: ____________________

राम राम जय

सीता राम

rāma rāma

jaya

sītā rāma

॥ राम राम जय सीता राम ॥

rāma rāma jaya sītā rāma .108.

Chant the Holy-Name Rāma-Rāma, glory to Sītā-Rāma.

राम राम जय राजा राम - राम राम जय सीता राम
राम राम जय राजा राम - राम राम जय सीता राम
राम राम जय राजा राम - राम राम जय सीता राम

rāma rāma jaya rājā rāma - rāma rāma jaya sītā rāma
rāma rāma jaya rājā rāma - rāma rāma jaya sītā rāma
rāma rāma jaya rājā rāma - rāma rāma jaya sītā rāma

श्रीनामरामायणम

śrī nāma rāmāyaṇam

⌘⌘⌘⌘⌘⌘⌘⌘⌘⌘⌘⌘⌘⌘⌘⌘⌘⌘⌘⌘⌘⌘⌘⌘

-- बालकाण्डः -- bālakāṇḍaḥ --

|| शुद्धब्रह्मपरात्पर राम ||

śuddha brahma parāt para rāma .1.

Behold Rāma—of the nature of pure Braham, who is the Supreme-One, second to none.

|| कालात्मकपरमेश्वर राम ||

kālātmaka param eśvara rāma .2.

Behold Rāma—Sovereign Godhead, the embodiment of Eternal Time.

|| शेषतल्पसुखनिद्रित राम ||

śeṣa talpa sukha nidrita rāma .3.

Behold Rāma—who slumbers joyously on the bed made of serpent Shesha Naga.

|| ब्रह्माद्यमरप्रार्थित राम ||

brahmādy amara prār thita rāma .4.

Behold Rāma—whose Lotus Feet are venerated by Brahmmā and other divinities—with a view to attaining ever-lasting life.

|| चण्डकिरणकुलमण्डन राम ||

caṇḍa kiraṇa kula maṇḍana rāma .5.

Behold Rāma—the shining Jewel of the Solar-Dynasty.

|| श्रीमद्दशरथनन्दन राम ||

śrīmad daśaratha nandana rāma .6.

Behold Rāma—the illustrious Son of King Dashrath.

|| कौसल्यासुखवर्धन राम ||

kausalyā sukha vardhana rāma .7.

Behold Rāma—who exceedingly amplifies His mother Kausalyā's joy.

|| विश्वामित्रप्रियधन राम ||

viśvāmitra priya dhana rāma .8.

Behold Rāma—the very precious treasure of Sage Vishwāmitra.

|| घोरताटकाघातक राम ||

ghora tāṭakā ghātaka rāma .9.

Behold Rāma—Slayer of Tādaka, the terrible fiend.

|| मारीचादिनिपातक राम ||

mārīcādi nipātaka rāma .10.

Behold Rāma—who wrought the downfall of Māricha and other Demons.

|| कौशिकमखसंरक्षक राम ||

kauśika makha saṁ rakṣaka rāma .11.

Behold Rāma—the Guardian of the Yagya of Sage Vishwāmitra.

|| श्रीमदहल्योद्धारक राम ||

śrīmad ahalyoddhāraka rāma .12.

Behold Rāma—as He imparts redemption to the venerable Ahalyā.

|| गौतममुनिसंपूजित राम ||

gautama muni saṁ pūjita rāma .13.

Behold Rāma—being worshipped by Muni Gautam.

|| सुरमुनिवरगणसंस्तुत राम ||

sura muni vara gaṇa saṁstuta rāma .14

Behold Rāma—who is ever praised by the gods and hosts of sages

|| नाविकधाविकमृदुपद राम ||

nāvika dhāvika mṛdu pada rāma .15.

Behold Rāma—whose gentle feet are being washed by the Boatman.

|| मिथिलापुरजनमोहक राम ||

mithilā pura jana mohaka rāma .16.

Behold Rāma—the Lordly prince who has so captivated the citizenry of Mithila.

|| विदेहमानसरञ्जक राम ||

videha mānasa rañjaka rāma .17.

Behold Rāma—who has enhanced the glory of King Janaka.

|| त्र्यंबककार्मुखभञ्जक राम ||

tryaṁbaka kārmukha bhañjaka rāma .18.

Behold Rāma—as He breaks the Bow of the Three-Eyed Shiva.

|| सीतार्पितवरमालिक राम ||

sītārpita vara mālika rāma .19.

Behold Sītā—who offers Her victory-garland to Rāma in matrimony.

|| कृतवैवाहिककौतुक राम ||

kṛta vaivāhika kautuka rāma .20.

Behold Rāma—as He enacts the sport of marriage ceremony.

|| भार्गवदर्पविनाशक राम ||

bhārgava darpa vināśaka rāma .21.

Behold Rāma—now seen destroying the pride of Parshurāma.

|| श्रीमदयोध्यापालक राम ||

śrīmad ayodhyā pālaka rāma .22.

Behold Rāma—the Lord-God, Ayodhya's Empyreal Sovereign.

राम राम जय राजा राम - राम राम जय सीता राम

rāma rāma jaya rājā rāma - rāma rāma jaya sītā rāma

Sing the glories of the Almighty—Raja Rāma; chant the Holy-Name Rāma-Rāma, Sītā-Rāma.

-- अयोध्याकाण्डः -- ayodhyākāṇḍaḥ --

|| अगणितगुणगणभूषित राम ||

agaṇita guṇa gaṇa bhūṣita rāma .23.

Behold Rāma—who is graced with immeasurable virtues.

|| अवनीतनयाकामित राम ||

avanī tanayā kāmita rāma .24.

Behold Rāma—the heart's desire of Sītā: Daughter-of-the-Earth.

|| राकाचन्द्रसमानन राम ||

rākā candra samānana rāma .25.

Behold Rāma—whose resplendent face is like the full Moon.

|| पितृवाक्याश्रितकानन राम ||

pitṛ vākyāśrita kānana rāma .26.

Behold Rāma—who leaves for exile to the forest in order to honor His father's words.

|| प्रियगुहविनिवेदितपद राम ||

priya guha vinivedita pada rāma .27.

Behold Rāma—unto whose holy feet Guha offers himself up as a cherished devotee.

|| तत्क्षालितनिजमृदुपद राम ||

tat kṣālita nija mṛdu pada rāma .28.

Behold Rāma—whose gentle feet Guha has the good fortune to lave.

|| भरद्वाजमुखानन्दक राम ||

bharadvāja mukh ānandaka rāma .29.

Behold Rāma—whose presence makes Sage Bharadwaja face lighten up with supreme joy.

|| चित्रकूटाद्रिनिकेतन राम ||

citra kūṭādri niketana rāma .30.

Behold Rāma—making Mount Chitrakut His habitat in the woods.

|| दशरथसन्ततचिन्तित राम ||

daśaratha santata cintita rāma .31.

Behold Rāma—ever mindful of Dashratha, His father, during the exile.

|| कैकेयीतनयार्थित राम ||

kaikeyī tanay ārthita rāma .32.

Behold Rāma—being eagerly besought by the son of Kaikayi to come return to His Kingdom.

|| विरचितनिजपितृकर्मक राम ||

viracita nija pitṛ karmaka rāma .33.

Behold Rāma—seen performing the last rites of his sire—King Dashrath.

|| भरतार्पितनिजपादुक राम ||

bharatārpita nija pāduka rāma .34.

Behold Rāma—as He bestows His own Padukā to brother Bharat.

राम राम जय राजा राम - राम राम जय सीता राम

rāma rāma jaya rājā rāma - rāma rāma jaya sītā rāma

Sing the glories of the Almighty—Raja Rāma; chant the Holy-Name Rāma-Rāma, Sītā-Rāma.

-- अरण्यकाण्डः -- aranyakāṇḍaḥ --

|| दण्डकावनजनपावन राम ||

daṇḍakā vana jana pāvana rāma .35.

Behold Rāma—who has sanctified the Dandak Forest and the habitants therein.

|| दुष्टविराधविनाशन राम ||

duṣṭa virādha vināśana rāma .36.

Behold Rāma—who has destroyed Viradha the wicked demon.

|| शरभङ्गसुतीक्ष्णार्चित राम ||

śarabhaṅga sutīkṣṇ ārcita rāma .37.

Behold Rāma—being worshipped by the sages Sharabhang and Sutīkshan.

|| अगस्त्यानुग्रहवर्धित राम ||

agastyānugraha vardhita rāma .38.

Behold Rāma—augmented with the blessings and grace of sage Agastya.

|| गृध्राधिपसंसेवित राम ||

gṛdhr ādhipa saṁ sevita rāma .39.

Behold Rāma—being honored by Jatāyu, the vulture-king.

|| पञ्चवटीतटसुस्थित राम ||

pañca vaṭī taṭa susthita rāma .40.

Behold Rāma—dwelling on the banks of the river at Panchavati.

|| शूर्पणखार्त्तिविधायक राम ||.

śūrpa ṇakhārtti vidhāyaka rāma .41.

Behold Rāma—as He visits punishment upon Surpanakha for her wicked deeds.

|| खरदूषणमुखसूदक राम ||

khara dūṣaṇa mukha sūdaka rāma .42.

Behold Rāma—seen effacing demons Khara and Dushana from the world.

|| सीताप्रियहरिणानुग राम ||

sītā priya hariṇ ānuga rāma .43.

Behold Rāma—as He pursues the deer which Sītā has wished for herself.

|| मारीचार्तिकृदाशुग राम ||

mārīcārti kṛdāśuga rāma .44.

Behold Rāma—who visits pain with an arrow upon Marich for his faulty deeds.

|| विनष्टसीतान्वेषक राम ||

vinaṣṭa sītā nveṣaka rāma .45.

Behold Rāma—seen earnestly searching for Sītā, His beloved, who is found missing.

|| गृध्राधिपगतिदायक राम ||

gṛdhrā dhipa gati dāyaka rāma .46.

Behold Rāma—imparting emancipation to Jatāyu, the vulture-king.

|| शबरीदत्तफलाशन राम ||

śabarī datta phalā śana rāma .47.

Behold Rāma—partaking of the fruit offerings made by the woman sage Shabarī.

|| कबन्धबाहुच्छेदन राम ||

kabandha bāhu cchedana rāma .48.

Behold Rāma—severing the arms of Kabandh, the monster fiend.

राम राम जय राजा राम - राम राम जय सीता राम

rāma rāma jaya rājā rāma - rāma rāma jaya sītā rāma

Sing the glories of the Almighty—Raja Rāma; chant the Holy-Name Rāma-Rāma, Sītā-Rāma.

-- किष्किन्धाकाण्डः -- kiṣkindhākāṇḍaḥ --

|| हनुमत्सेवितनिजपद राम ||

hanumat sevita nija pada rāma .49.

Behold Rāma—King of Kings, whose Holy Feet are being served by Hanumān, the monkey chief.

|| नतसुग्रीवाभीष्टद राम ||

nata sugrīv ābhīṣ ṭada rāma .50.

Behold Rāma—granting the prayers of Sugrīva, who has arrived bowing to Him, seeking refuge.

|| गर्वितवालिसंहारक राम ||

garvita vāli saṁ hāraka rāma .51.

Behold Rāma—who has put to death Vāli, the haughty monkey-king.

|| वानरदूतप्रेषक राम ||

vānara dūta preṣaka rāma .52.

Behold Rāma—who has sent monkeys as emissaries in search of Sītā.

|| हितकरलक्ष्मणसंयुत राम ||

hita kara lakṣmaṇa saṁyuta rāma .53.

Behold Rāma—with Lakshman dwelling alongside Him, serving devotedly.

राम राम जय राजा राम - राम राम जय सीता राम

rāma rāma jaya rājā rāma - rāma rāma jaya sītā rāma

Sing the glories of the Almighty—Raja Rāma; chant the Holy-Name Rāma-Rāma, Sītā-Rāma.

-- सुन्दरकाण्डः -- sundarakāṇḍaḥ --

|| कपिवरसन्ततसंस्मृत राम ||

kapi vara santata saṁ smṛta rāma .54.

Behold Rāma—who is continually thought upon by Hanumān, the most-excellent amongst the monkeys.

|| तद्गतिविघ्नध्वंसक राम ||

tad gati vighna dhvaṁ saka rāma .55.

Behold Rāma—as He removes all impediments & obstacles to the swiftness of Hanumān's rapid speed.

|| सीताप्राणाधारक राम ||

sītā prāṇ ādhāraka rāma .56.

Behold Rāma—the support and sustenance of the life of Sītā in captivity.

|| दुष्टदशाननदूषित राम ||

duṣṭa daśānana dūṣita rāma .57.

Behold Rāma—being affronted & marred by the wicked Ten-Headed Rāvan.

|| शिष्टहनूमद्भूषित राम ||

śiṣṭa hanūmad bhūṣita rāma .58.

Behold Rāma—praised & graced by the honorable Hanumān.

|| सीतावेदितकाकावन राम ||

sītā vedita kākā vana rāma .59.

Behold Rāma—as He hears of the Kakasur incident in woods which was conveyed to Him by Shrī Sītā.

|| कृतचूडामणिदर्शन राम ||

kṛta cūḍā maṇi darśana rāma .60.

Behold Rāma—beholding the head-crest chudāmani of Shrī Sītā.

|| कपिवरवचनाश्वासित राम ||

kapi vara vacan āśvāsita rāma .61.

Behold Rāma—being comforted by the words of Shrī Hanumān, the wisest amongst the monkeys.

राम राम जय राजा राम - राम राम जय सीता राम

rāma rāma jaya rājā rāma - rāma rāma jaya sītā rāma

Sing the glories of the Almighty—Raja Rāma; chant the Holy-Name Rāma-Rāma, Sītā-Rāma.

-- युद्धकाण्डः -- yuddhakāṇḍaḥ --

|| रावणनिधनप्रस्थित राम ||

rāvaṇa nidhana prasthita rāma .62.

Behold Rāma—as He sallies forth to decimate Rāvan, the demon king.

|| वानरसैन्यसमावृत राम ||

vānara sainya sam āvṛta rāma .63.

Behold Rāma—accompanied by the army of bears and monkeys.

|| शोषितसरिदीशार्थित राम ||

śoṣita saridīś ārthita rāma .64.

Behold Rāma— being importuned by the king of oceans when He asks It to make way—and then makes ready to dry up the sea.

|| विभीष्णाभयदायक राम ||

vibhīṣṇ ābhaya dāyaka rāma .65.

Behold Rāma—who confers fearlessness upon Vibhīshan who has come seeking sanctuary.

|| पर्वतसेतुनिबन्धक राम ||

parvata setu niban dhaka rāma .66.

Behold Rāma—who has spanned a bridge of rocks across the ocean.

|| कुम्भकर्णशिरश्छेदक राम ||

kumbha karṇa śiraś chedaka rāma .67.

Behold Rāma—as He beheads Kumbhkaran in combat.

|| राक्षससङ्घविमर्दक राम ||

rākṣasa saṅgha vimardaka rāma .68.

Behold Rāma—crushing the army of demons on the battleground.

|| अहिमहिरावणचारण राम ||

ahi mahi rāvaṇa cāraṇa rāma .69.

Behold Rāma—upon whom Ahi-Mahi Rāvana spied taking the guise of musician.

|| संहृतदशमुखरावण राम ||

saṁ hṛta daśa mukha rāvaṇa rāma .70.

Behold Rāma—as He kills the Ten-Headed Rāvan in the battlefield.

|| विधिभवमुखसुरसंस्तुत राम ||

vidhi bhava mukha sura saṁ stuta rāma .71

Behold Rāma—being worshiped by Brahmmā, Shiva and other Divinities.

|| स्वस्थितदशरथवीक्षित राम ||

svasthita daśaratha vīkṣita rāma .72.

Behold Rāma—whose divine deeds are being witnessed by father Dashratha from the Heavens.

|| सीतादर्शनमोदित राम ||

sītā darśana modita rāma .73.

Behold Rāma—as He beholds with delight Shrī Sītā after the battle is won.

|| अभिषिक्तविभीषणनत राम ||

abhi ṣikta vibhīṣaṇa nata rāma .74.

Behold Rāma—being reverentially saluted by Vibhīshan after his own corronation.

|| पुष्पकयानारोहण राम ||

puṣpaka yān ārohaṇa rāma .75.

Behold Rāma—while He boards the aerial Pushpaka Vimana to return to Ayodhya, His Kingdom.

|| भरद्वाजादिनिषेवण राम ||

bharadvāj ādi niṣevaṇa rāma .76.

Behold Rāma—being served by sage Bharadwaja and the other sages.

|| भरतप्राणप्रियकर राम ||

bharata prāṇa priyakara rāma .77.

Behold Rāma—who brings joy to Bharta's life upon His return.

|| साकेतपुरीभूषण राम ||

sāketa purī bhūṣaṇa rāma .78.

Behold Rāma—the adornment of the city of Saket.

|| सकलस्वीयसमानस राम ||

sakala svīya sam ānasa rāma .79.

Behold Rāma—being welcomed and venerated by the citizenry of Ayodhyā.

|| रत्नलसत्पीठास्थित राम ||

ratnala satpīṭh āsthita rāma .80.

Behold Rāma—seated on the Royal Throne embellished with shining jewels.

|| पट्टाभिषेकालंकृत राम ||

paṭṭ ābhiṣek ālaṁkṛta rāma .81.

Behold Rāma—adorned with the Royal Robes and Crown upon His coronation.

|| पार्थिवकुलसम्मानित राम ||

pārthiva kula sammānita rāma .82.

Behold Rāma— being honoured by the Assembly of Kings

|| विभीषणार्पितरङ्गक राम ||

vibhīṣaṇ ārpita raṅgaka rāma .83.

Behold Rāma—as He confers the idol of Shrī Ranganātha to Vibhishana.

|| कीशकुलानुग्रहकर राम ||

kīśa kul ānugraha kara rāma .84.

Behold Rāma— showering His benediction upon the host of Monkeys.

|| सकलजीवसंरक्षक राम ||

sakala jīva saṁ rakṣaka rāma .85.

Behold Rāma—the Guardian of all beings.

|| समस्तलोकाधारक राम ||

samasta lokādhāraka rāma .86.

Behold Rāma—the Sustainer of all the worlds.

राम राम जय राजा राम - राम राम जय सीता राम

rāma rāma jaya rājā rāma - rāma rāma jaya sītā rāma

Sing the glories of the Almighty—Raja Rāma; chant the Holy-Name Rāma-Rāma, Sītā-Rāma.

|| आगत मुनिगण संस्तुत राम ||

āgata muni gaṇa saṁ stuta rāma .87.

Behold Rāma—being revered by the visiting host of Munis.

|| विश्रुतदशकण्ठोद्भव राम ||

viśruta daśa kaṇṭh odbhava rāma .88.

Behold Rāma—as He hears the story of origin of the Ten-Faced Rāvan.

|| सितालिङ्गननिर्वृत राम ||

sitā liṅgana nirvṛta rāma .89.

Behold Rāma—living happily, united with Sītā.

|| नीतिसुरक्षितजनपद राम ||

nīti surakṣita jana pada rāma .90.

Behold Rāma—who protects His Sovereignity through Dharma—the moral-precept.

|| विपिनत्याजितजनकज राम ||

vipina tyājita jana kaja rāma .91.

Behold Rāma—who has to abandon the daughter of Janak into the woods.

|| कारितलवणासुरवध राम ||

kārita lavaṇāsura vadha rāma .92.

Behold Rāma—as He brings about destruction of the Lavanasura Demon.

|| स्वर्गतशम्बुक संस्तुत राम ||

svargata śambuka saṁstuta rāma .93.

Behold Rāma—being praised by Shambuka, whom He sent to the Heavens.

|| स्वतनयकुशलवनन्दित राम ||

sva tanaya kuśa lava nandita rāma .94.

Behold Rāma—jubilant by the sight of His sons Kusha and Lava.

|| अश्वमेधक्रतुदीक्षित राम ||

aśva medha kratu dīkṣita rāma .95.

Behold Rāma—performing the sacrifices of Ashwamedha Yagya, proper to a King.

|| कालावेदितसुरपद राम ||

kālā vedita sura pada rāma .96.

Behold Rāma— as He is reminded of His Divine-Abode from Kāla, the mighty Time.

|| आयोध्यकजनमुक्तित राम ||

āyodhyaka jana muktita rāma .97.

Behold Rāma—conferring salvation upon all the inhabitants of Ayodhyā.

|| विधिमुखविभुदानन्दक राम ||

vidhi mukha vibhud ānandaka rāma .98.

Behold Rāma—who causes the faces of Brahmmā and other gods to brighten up with joy.

|| तेजोमयनिजरूपक राम ||

tejo maya nija rūpaka rāma .99.

Behold Rāma—who has assumed His own resplendent Divine-Form—fiery and gleaming.

|| संसृतिबन्धविमोचक राम ||

saṁsṛti bandha vimocaka rāma .100.

Behold Rāma—who releases one from all the bondages of worldly existence.

|| धर्मस्थापनतत्पर राम ||

dharma sthāpana tatpara rāma .101.

Behold Rāma—ever ready to establish Dharma on Earth.

|| भक्तिपरायणमुक्तिद राम ||

bhakti parāyaṇa muktida rāma .102.

Behold Rāma—giving salvation to Devotees that are completely dependent upon Him in thoughts, words, deeds.

|| सर्वचराचरपालक राम ||

sarva car ācara pālaka rāma .103.

Behold Rāma—the Guardian of all beings, moving and non-moving.

|| सर्वभवामयवारक राम ||

sarva bhavā maya vāraka rāma .104.

Behold Rāma—who takes His Devotees beyond the worldly dualities.

॥ वैकुण्ठालयसंस्थित राम ॥
vaikuṇṭh ālaya saṁ sthita rāma .105.
Behold Rāma—ever established in His Divine Abode at Vaikuntha.

॥ नित्यानन्दपदस्थित राम ॥
nityā nanda pada sthita rāma .106.
Behold Rāma—forever established as the Divine Godhead of Eternal Bliss.

॥ राम राम जय राजा राम ॥
rāma rāma jaya rājā rāma .107.
Sing the glories of the Almighty—Raja Rāma.

॥ राम राम जय सीता राम ॥
rāma rāma jaya sītā rāma .108.
Chant the Holy-Name Rāma-Rāma; glory to Sītā-Rāma.

⌘⌘⌘

राम राम जय राजा राम - राम राम जय सीता राम rāma rāma jaya rājā rāma - rāma rāma jaya sītā rāma
राम राम जय राजा राम - राम राम जय सीता राम rāma rāma jaya rājā rāma - rāma rāma jaya sītā rāma
राम राम जय राजा राम - राम राम जय सीता राम rāma rāma jaya rājā rāma - rāma rāma jaya sītā rāma

⌘⌘⌘

(Author of the Original Sanskrit Hymn is: Shrī Lakshmanāchārya [Medieval Indian Saint]. Translator: Sushma)

Printed in the USA
CPSIA information can be obtained
at www.ICGtesting.com
CBHW080551121224
18872CB00015B/1129

9 781945 739309